When Anger Strikes

When Anger Strikes
By: O'Tia Prioleau

COPYRIGHT

O'Tia Prioleau

CHAPTER ONE:

JUST THE BEGINNING

BOOM! CRASH!

"Stop it Joseph, settle down please." said a woman with plentiful, long, black hair with skin that shined like a glazed donut in the sun. She wore a short light blue dress with black strapped six-inch heels.

The class was in the middle of reading hour when this dispute happened.

Joseph stood there, frozen, with hatred in his face holding a chair raised in the air above a child with a fro of curly blonde hair. As the other students observed on their feet in concern for poor little Mike, Joseph was aiming to drop the chair on him. "Ms. Vowel," Mike cried as he sat on the floor in fear and lifted his arms in a struggling attempt to block the seat from hitting him.

"HE TOOK MY HEADPHONES!" said Joseph, turning towards Mrs. Vowel, their seventh-grade teacher, as Mike covered his ears to avoid Joseph's vocals, "I can't allow Mike to take ownership of my things, it is not fair."

Joseph was a chunky boy with short brown hair, his body resembled the shape of an egg. He wore a yellow and blue striped short-sleeve shirt with khaki shorts and brown

Sperry, which he basically wore every day.

Joseph was just ticked off by the littlest of

things and did not have many friends, but his

grades were always on point, A's that is. His

parents knew about his condition, but never

took it at heart. Whether he was at school or at

home, it was still a problem.

"I didn't take nothing; I don't know what you are

talking about you FREAK...GET OUT OF MY

WAY!" said Mike as he stood to his feet

pushing Joseph out of his path to leave the

classroom.

Mike was a tall skinny boy with freckles all over

his face. He wore a black leather jacket with a

white t-shirt and blue jeans with black shoes,

almost looking like a grease character. He

always got in trouble, bad grades, ISS was his place.

"No one is leaving till I say class is over." Mrs. Vowel said forcibly.

The bell rang and it was time to go, but as far as the kids knew; the bell didn't dismiss them, Mrs. Vowel did.

"Well, what is the bell for then?" A girl with sass, class and attitude said; her name was Sunny, originally from Alabama, curly redhead who always did her homework. Her hair was up in a bun, she wore a gorgeous black sparkly dress with white three-inch heels, and white gloves like she was going to have tea with the queen. All she was missing was a tiara on her head.

"Excuse me?" Mrs. Vowel says, "The rest of you can go except for Mike, Sunny and Joseph."

The students left the classroom empty with only the four remaining. Mrs. Vowel walked over to Sunny first who was standing by the open classroom door.

Sunny decides to question Mrs. Vowel as she approaches her, "Why do you have to pick on me?" she says with poise in her voice.

"I know I'm not just hearing things about Sunny, but your comment was uncalled for. I do not appreciate it, okay. I know you do not want me to meet with your parents, so that means you need to know how to respect your elders when they say one thing, you do not say another. Do you understand?" says Mrs. Vowel with authority and understanding.

Meanwhile, Mike and Joseph sat there five desks apart. Mike on the right side and Joseph on the left. Mike chose to look at the board in front of him while Joseph fixed his eyes on Mike, looking him straight in the cheek with anger in him.

"Okay, I understand Mrs. Vowel, I am so sorry, I didn't mean it in that way, honestly." Sunny says apologetically.

"Good, you can go now."

Mrs. Vowel dismisses Sunny and immediately goes to Mike and Joseph. She passes Joseph and takes a seat at the desk in the center of them. She places her hands together in front of her and says with passion in her voice as she stares straight at the front of the classroom: "Mike, do you or do you not have Joseph's headphones?"

"NO!" Mike says in frustration.

Before Mrs. Vowel could respond to that, Joseph dramatically jumps out of his seat and screams towards the two saying, "YES HE DID CHECK HIS BAG!" motioning to a green backpack in the far-left corner by the door.

"SIT down…please. I can handle this Joseph. Mike go get your bag for me…," Mrs. Vowel is talking then Mike interrupts her.

"But Mrs. Vowel…" Mike interjects.

With the force of irritation, Mrs. Vowel slams her fists on the desks and says, "NOW!" looking at Mike with a bitter pill face.

Mike walks over to his backpack and opens it. Then he walks over to Mrs. Vowel slowly holding the bag wide open. She peaks her hand inside to feel for the headphones, then makes up her mind to stick her whole arm in, but still there was no sign of the headphones.

"I do not see them." concluded Mrs. Vowel.

"That's because I did not take them." Mike informs her. The three walk outside to the lockers and Joseph opens his. They find that Joseph left his headphones in his locker and Mike never took them.

"Mike, go back and take a seat in the classroom please, I'll deal with you in a minute." she says as she puts her hands on her hips with eyes locked on Joseph.

Mike walks away in despair.

"I can't believe you got into a fight again for no good reason. You practically injured another student because you thought he had your headphones. Go to the office now please, I need to deal with Mike first." Mrs. Vowel said with no allowance of Joseph's input.

Mike went home that day with a bruised arm. All that fuss made Mrs. Vowel call Joseph's parents in for a parent teacher conference. When the school day ended, his parents arrived to find him sitting outside the classroom. Mr. Louis, like his son, had brown hair and was a big tall, important looking man who worked in the office business. He was top of the line market manager for the Hotel industry; which was their family business. Mrs.

Louis was also a brunette who loved palates and runs in the park, but was not the best cook. On the other hand, she was a therapist who loved her work. Mrs. Louis had great clients and not so great clients, but she did not mind.

She wore a short dress, green on top and black half way to the bottom; added a black blazer with some black closed toe shoes and finished it off with some green dangling jewelry. She wore her hair straight down like she usually does, but she did not wear any makeup, nor lipstick. Her husband, Mr. Louis, wore the usual suit; black and white-collar shirt with a green tie. Even though they work separate jobs they still matched at times to show their love for one another.

"Hello Mister and Misses Louis." Mrs. Vowel goes to shake Joseph's parent's hands, "I'm glad you can make it again on such short notice." The Louises took their seats in two chairs across from Mrs. Vowel.

Joseph sat in the hallway in the chair outside Mrs. Vowel's classroom in melancholy because it was his tenth conference alone that semester, he knew he was in trouble.

"I think you know why I asked for your attendance, right?" Mrs. Vowel began.

Mrs. Louis answered, "Yes ma'am Misses Vowel. Our son Joseph has been acting out again, I assure you we will handle it."

"No, no, it is not your doing, it is just that, he... well…. Joseph has an anger issue. I know you denied this before, but I feel that we can help him a lot better if...you know...he was in our special needs program or maybe anger management. I think he'll succeed in those two things and use it to his best ability." Mrs. Vowel says and looks up at Mr and Misses Louis with great value in her eyes and slides out several folders titled: We Care! and Ask Me Why? With both Louis' faces in disbelief, Mr. Louis finally says, "You think this is the best way to help MY son?" immediately standing to his feet. "YOU KNOW WHY WE DENIED THIS BEFORE. MY son is not a retard." Mrs. Vowel interrupts him, "Mr. Louis, please do not use the R word here."

"My husband can use whatever word he wants." Mrs. Louis stands, "You know what, we do not need this." Points at Mrs. Vowel, "we do not need YOU," Throws her hands up and yells to the ceiling, "WE DO NOT NEED NONE OF YOU! THIS IS A DISGRACE!"

Mr. Louis throws the folders to the floor, puts his hands on his hips with annoyance and points vigorously on her desk, "IN FACT," motions to the door to acknowledge Joseph, "MY SON is one of the smartest ones at this school. COME ON HONEY, LETS GO!" Mr. Louis yells as he marches out.

The two take their son home, never to return to that school again.

CHAPTER TWO:

TIME FOR A CHANGE

Monday morning rolls around, Joseph is up and ready for school. Even though his anger was a problem, keeping his room clean was not. He kept his room organized in a strange fashion; Joseph had labels for everything in his room. His underwear, which was all white, went in the first drawer of his dresser. Next came his short sleeve shirt in the second drawer. Then came his short khaki pants in the drawer below and finally came his white socks neatly laid out pair by pair on top of each other in the last drawer. Joseph's shoes were in the closet and because they were Sperry's he only had three pairs of them. Every morning he would get ready in the exact same order: undies, shirt, pants, socks, and shoes. Not only was his clothes and shoes organized, so was his entire room, everything from his books on his shelf to his toothbrush in his bathroom. His mother already knew his routine, but did not bother with it because she knew his condition and his father never had time to go into his room to see the labels because of his dedication to work so he wasn't aware of much about his son.

Joseph goes downstairs and witnesses his mom in a messy kitchen wearing her long-sleeved, polka-dot, two-piece pajamas with her pink kiss the cook apron preparing breakfast for Joseph: a bowl of Captain Crunch and for her; Special K fruit and yogurt. She nearly burned down the kitchen trying to make pancakes. The sad part is that she did not even make her own batter; she used instant pancakes which were all over her face and apron. She welcomes Joseph with open arms…

"Good morning sweetie."

Walking to the kitchen with his red book bag to hug his mom, "Good morning mom," he shakes her hand instead to avoid the pancakes from reaching his clothes. "Why didn't you wake me

up? I'm going to be late for school, come on."
says Joseph as he rushes to the front door.
Mr. Louis walks in from upstairs wearing a full-on suit with just a plain black tie. He goes in to pour himself a hot cup of coffee, "You are not going to be late, because you are not going." Joseph confronts his father, "WHAT! Are you serious?"

"Yes, I'm serious son," Mr. Louis says as he takes a sip of his coffee. He walks over to his wife and gives her a side hug with a kiss. "I'm going to stop for breakfast on the way to work. Honey, can you tell him what is going on? I'm going to be late." Mr. Louis says in a scamper way as he rushes out almost tripping over the rug in front of the door.

Mrs. Louis takes hold of Joseph's right hand with disappointment on his face and walks him to the living room and as they take their seat she tells Joseph, "Your father is right," she pauses in thought, "...but what he really means is that you are going to be homeschooled sweetheart."

"Homeschooled? Why can't I go back to normal school?" Joseph says with suspense. He turns to his mom and looks at her with distraught emotion, "Are you going to be my home school teacher?" Joseph asked.

"Yes, I am," Mrs. Louis says with joy.

She was barely home for school. Homeschool turned out to be a struggle for Joseph. He was out of school for at least four weeks now and his mom has yet to teach him a thing. She was busy with work as usual. Some days Joseph would come with her and other days he would stay home and just watch TV. When he would go with his mom to work he would often get bored and agitated. You would think that Mrs. Louis, being a therapist and all, would be able to help her son deal with his anger issues, but other clients keep her busy. All she could do when he would get angry was let him be and he would eventually cool off. Joseph was not allowed to go with his father to work mainly because he worked at a hotel and his father would not be able to keep an eye on him. Being home was no fun because often he was lonely and the only time Joseph was not alone was when his neighbor, Terry Jones, was around after school. Even though she attended a different school than Joseph they were best friends. She went to a private school down the street. She is top of her class as well as Joseph was. She is an African American girl with natural curly black hair. She traveled a lot during the summer because of her mother's profession, so she knew more than English. Her mom is an activist and wrote lots of novels. Her father is a judge who often worked some night shifts, so when her mother was away and her father was working she would come home to an empty house like Joseph did.

"Hey Joe!" Terry calls as she walks up the steps to Joseph's front door to knock. She was a tall, skinny girl who wore her school uniform, blue-collar shirt and tan skirt. Terry also wore black glasses and shoes with blue socks and her hair was in pigtails.

Joseph opened the door and greeted Terry with a smile. "Terry, hey what's happening, how's school?"

"Ohhhhh, let me tell you…. It's just great. It's FANTASTIC" she says sarcastically as she flops on Joseph's coach.

Joseph chuckles.

As he and Terry watched TV his mother calls, Joseph got up to go to the kitchen to get water from the fridge for Terry and himself in time to hear the ring.

"Hello sweetie, sorry I can't make it home exactly on time today because I have been going over a lot of my clients, but I will be home later tonight around eight. I love you and you can order a pizza if you would like. Oh, and hello Terry!"

"Hey mom and Terry says hi. See you when you get home." Joseph says.

"Love You."

"Love you too." Joseph replys.

Joseph ordered his usual--bacon, chicken, garlic with ranch on the side. His mom often did this a lot, so he was used to it. While his mom never came home to teach him, Terry taught him everything she learned each school day.

Another day came and Joseph got an idea as he stood in the Kitchen on a Friday night while Terry sat on the couch turning through channels on the TV wearing her schoolgirl outfit, "What am I supposed to eat now? I can't believe I'm saying this, but I'm so tired of pizza." Joseph told Terry from the kitchen, but she was too distracted from the TV to know what Joseph was talking about.

"Did you say something Joe?" She asks, "It's probably nothing." Terry says to herself.

It was almost 5, which meant it was almost dinner time. Joseph asked himself, "What is the easiest dish to make?" Casserole came to his head. "How about I make a casserole. Aunt Regina makes them all of the time, so it shouldn't be hard." Terry, still glued to Henry Danger, paid him no mind as he preheated the oven to 300 and immediately started looking in the fridge. He grabs the shredded cheese and the sandwich turkey meat, "It needs cheese and this turkey meat can replace the chicken she used." He grabbed the milk as well, "I remember seeing Aunt Regina pouring milk." Then he looked for the broccoli and tater-tots in the freezer. "They have to be in here."

Terry enters the kitchen still with her focus on the TV watching Henry and Ray transform into their superhero selves, she says, "I think I heard you speaking, were you talking to me?," She pauses when she approaches Joseph and turns to find his butt sticking out of the freezer, "What are you doing?" she asks in a laughing manner.

Joseph finds that there is only half a bag of broccoli and only ten tater-tots left, so he decides to use what he has.

Turning around to Terry as he sets the ingredients down on the counter, he says, "Oh, I'm trying to make us dinner, I'm making a casserole." He just mixed everything together in a medium white bowl, except for the tater-tots, and poured it in a white, glass dish. He puts the tater-tots on top and sets it in the oven. "Okay, I'll give it forty minutes and then I'll check on it."

"Great, want to learn algebra now?" Terry asks.

"Yeah, sure." Joseph says as he sets the oven timer to forty minutes and walks to the kitchen table with Terry to learn math.

Forty minutes have passed and the oven timer goes off while they are having a problem. Joseph goes to check on the casserole and hears the lock to the front door being opened; it was his mother.

"Hey Joseph and Terry, what are you up to, mm mm hmm something smells good, what is it?" Mrs. Louis asked.

Closing the oven Joseph answers his mom saying, "It's my broccoli casserole, it's not done yet though, it's almost done." Joseph walks back to his seat at the table.

"Okay, your father is on his way in." Mrs. Louis says as she sits down on the couch and sees the theme song for Drake and Josh playing as she picks up the remote to search the show NCIS.

"Oh hello Mrs. Louis, how was your day?" Terry says from the kitchen table with a greeting in her voice as she continues her studies with Joseph.

"Great, but excessively tiring." Mrs. Louis says as she removes her black heels and cardigan. She wore a black doll collar and full on red dress with red circled dangling earrings. When she clicked on her show, instantly, her husband entered.

"Hey honey, I'm home. Ha-ha I've always wanted to say that." Mr. Louis says as he accompanies his wife on the couch and greets her with a kiss.

"JOSEPH!!!, where are you son?" Mr. Louis says, looking around as Mrs. Louis continues to watch her show.

Joseph walks into the living room, "I was in the kitchen dad. Terry is here as well."

"Hello Mr. Louis!" Terry says with her hand raised to the sky so Mr. Louis can see.

"Oh," Looking back, stretching to see Terry he says," Hey Terry girl, dang, you got our house smelling good, I thought I smelled something, I was thinking it was my wife here ha-ha." He gets up from the couch in confidence and makes his way to the kitchen. "I got scared for a second." Mr. Louis walks into the kitchen with his son. "What have you prepared for me to eat Terry?"

Terry looks at Mr. Louis in confusion. "Dad, I made dinner. It's a broccoli casserole. MOM IT'S READY!!!" Joseph joyfully sings.

All four gathered around the dining room table and Mrs. Louis began to say a prayer.

"Lord, thank you for this meal that we are about to receive. I pray that…"

Mr. Louis interrupts," It does not kill us ha-ha"

Terry begins to laugh and friendly elbows Joseph to let him know it was a joke. "It was a joke." Terry whispers to Joseph. Joseph looks at her and hesitates and then gives a small chuckle. "OH, AHHH HAHAHAHA, GOOD ONE DAD" Joseph says.

"George." Mrs. Louis says as she kicks her husband from under the table.

Mr. Louis feels the kick and turns to his wife with a, "What? It was a joke." Mr. Louis claims. "Joseph laughed, see it was a joke, sorry I didn't mean to hurt your feelings. You know what son; I am going to enjoy this meal."

"It was mom, see I laughed" Joseph tries to convince his mom as Terry nods her head in agreement.

Mrs. Louis looks strenuously at the three and says, "Only because Terry told you," looking at Joseph with sincere in her voice, "you know what, never mind, we can just enjoy this wonderful meal you have prepared for us," looking at her husband, "but first let me finish the prayer with no interruptions please.

"I'll finish it," Mr. Louis says as Mrs. Louis smiles and bows her head in prayer. "I pray that this meal brings us joy and greatness. Amen."

 "Amen." They all lift their heads at the conclusion of the prayer. "In that case, let's eat." Joseph says.

The four relished the meal as they talked about their day.

"Mom, when am I going to start learning?" Joseph asked as he took a fork full of broccoli.

"Let me take this one Nancy." Mr. Louis answers, "Son, you learn every day, well you just learned how to make dinner. This broccoli casserole is one of the best I ever had, certainly better than Aunt Regina's."

"And I can continue to teach you what I learn from school too, I don't mind at all Joe." Terry says with a smile. Joseph smiles back and is interrupted by his mom.

"Joseph, you have an anger issue son and it is not fair to the other kids when you flip out on them for little things. I know we already told you this, but we need to start taking it seriously. You have a checkup next Friday with Dr. Grant and I took off work for it so I can take you." Mrs. Louis explains.

"Okay mom." Joseph says as he finishes the rest of his dinner in dismal.

Next week Friday came and it was checkup time. By this time Joseph managed to get his anger under control and since he was not surrounded by people all day like he usually was at school it was not much of a problem. This doctor's appointment was every two months and Mrs. Louis felt as though it helped, but Joseph did not feel any progress and that is why Mrs. Louis woke up that morning to no sign of Joseph.

"JOSEPH!!!" she says walking downstairs in her gray pants suit with black closed toe heels and hair in a bun and because she did not want to put on her contacts, she decided to wear her black framed glasses instead.

"JOSEPH, WHERE ARE YOU? Where is that kid?" she says as she grabs her black purse from the lamp stand by the couch. She walks around the house looking for Joseph.

"Okay, where is he?" she says to herself as she walks outside of the door. Still Yelling out for Joseph, she gets into her car and makes a right to look for him around the neighborhood knowing neither one of her neighbors was home. As she drives away, Joseph comes walking from the opposite direction with groceries and headphones in his ears walking towards the house. He walks in and does not notice the missing vehicle, he has forgotten all about the doctor's appointment and got up early to make his mother and him a nice breakfast of eggs, bacon, french toast and fruit. Joseph enjoyed making the casserole and the whole week he has been increasing in his baking and cooking skills by making many things, he has been watching a lot of the food network to help himself out. Terry told him about the grocery store that was only six blocks away. She witnessed him make chicken lasagna, shrimp, veggies and noodles, macaroni and meatballs, and so on, but for breakfast he would usually hold off and just eat his normal meal, cereal. His parents were not home for every dinner, but they got a taste of it for their lunch the next day.

Joseph calls out to his mother, "MOM!!!,

IT'S TIME TO WAKE UP….MOM???" Joseph

immediately runs upstairs to find his mother not

in her room and then he runs outside to see

the car missing. In panic Joseph calls his

mom's cell phone.

"Hey, mom!" Joseph greets her on the phone.

"JOSEPH!!!, WHERE ARE YOU?" Mrs. Louis

says in frustration.

"I'm home, where are you?" Joseph answers.

"OH MY GOSH!" Mrs. Louis says in confusion

and hangs up.

Joseph walks into the kitchen to start

making breakfast and a few moments go by

and his mother arrives. Joseph is beating eggs,

vanilla, and cinnamon into milk when he hears

the car pull up into the driveway; his mother enters in fury.

"WHERE WERE YOU?" she says in demand.

"Sorry, I went to get groceries for our breakfast." Joseph says as he comes from behind the kitchen counter mixing the bowl for the french toast wearing his mother's kiss the cook apron.

"Okayyyy…." *SIGHHH* Mrs. Louis says as she is trying to take a breather. "Well, I went looking for you because you were not where you were supposed to be, home, and because of that we are not going to make it in time for your doctor's appointment."

"I totally forgot about that, sorry mom, but I hope you enjoy what I am preparing for you to eat." Joseph says with no regret.

"Great, I can't wait." Mrs. Louis says in sarcasm as she sits down on the couch in relief. She turns on the TV and notices the two glasses of orange juice and the forks and spoons wrapped in napkins already set up on the coffee table.

The more Joseph practiced the more precise his cooking skills became. When he prepared the french toast, he made them the same so that when he lined them it was lined up perfectly. They each got three French toast, he poured the syrup in a zigzag motion and made it to where there was just enough syrup on top. Each got two pieces of bacon and when he made the eggs, he used three of them mixed with milk before he poured it into the pan to give it that fluffy look and taste. He mixed blueberries, cut up strawberries, and sliced up a banana and split it up into two small glass bowls. Joseph took the two bowls and brought them to the coffee table where his mom was and went back into the kitchen to get the two plates and walked over to the couch to park alongside his mother.

Mrs. Louis looks at the plate in shock, "Wow, Joseph…. All I can say is wow." She looks at him in disbelief.

With his mouth, full of toast and bacon he says, "Just wait till you taste it."

She cuts the French toast and takes a bite and that is the moment she realizes her son's talent.

"This is so good, oh my…. Joseph." She wipes her mouth with the napkin, "I know that being out of school has been hard, but I can see it benefited you in a way, right?”

“Yes, ma’am it did, I think I like cooking, I mean I’m so good at it, but if it is okay with you and dad I would like to go back to school. Maybe I can join Terry at her school.” Joseph says.

“I think that is a great idea, but a new school with new people, is that a good idea?” Mom says in concern.

“Well, I’ll have Terry with me, please mom.” Joseph sets his plate on the coffee table and gets on his knees and puts his hands together in prayer and continues to beg, “pleaseeeee, please please please please, pleaseeee!!!”

“ALRIGHT!!!, but we have to see if your dad is okay with it first.” Mom says as she continues to finish her breakfast.

Joseph puts his fist in the air in victory and says, "YES!!!" He sits down and continues to eat with a smile on his face.

Night time arrives and Mr. Louis walks in from a long day of work with a bag of Wendy's and his suitcase in his hands. He loosens his tie and walks into the kitchen to greet Joseph and his wife by the sink washing dishes. This time, Mr. Louis just wore a blue collared dress shirt with black dress pants and dress shoes. He kisses his wife on the cheek and taps his son's shoulder before he goes to the trash and throws his Wendy's bag away and resumes to walk upstairs to take a nap, but he is stopped by his son and wife's voice.

"Hey honey, how was your day?" Mrs. Louis says with delight. She was wearing a plain white T-shirt with her pink pajama bottoms.

"Great, darling yours…." Mr. Louis answers with his back facing his family, but interrupted by Joseph's eagerness.

"Yeah dad, hey, I have something to ask you really quick before you take your nap," Joseph says as he drops his drying cloth and scurries to his father's side. He was wearing the same clothes he wears every day, not having changed yet since this morning.

Mrs. Louis watches Joseph as her husband says, "Yes son, what is it?" Mr. Louis says as he turns around and raises his head with confusion on his face to his wife.

"Go on Joey, ask your dad what you asked me earlier today." Mrs. Louis says as she scrubs the residue from a white decorative glass plate. "Yes ma'am...ahhhh dad…" Mr. Louis looks down at Joseph as he continues to speak. "I was wondering if I could go back to school and I know you hate the idea of me being in the special needs program, so that is why I would like to go to Terry's school instead. How about that idea dad?" Joseph says in a back and forth motion with his head as he transitions from looking at his dad to mom and back at his dad again.

"Absolutely not." Mr. Louis says in disbelief and proceeds to go upstairs for his nap.

"WHAT! GEORGE GET BACK HERE!" Mrs. Louis yells as she pauses her dishwashing and sets the plate back into the soapy water and cleans her hands with Joseph's drying cloth only to join her husband upstairs in their bedroom. Joseph just stood in the kitchen in desolation. He could hear them arguing as he walked to continue his mom's dishwashing. He heard his mom say things like, "What is your problem?" and "Listen to me." He heard his dad say, "Because I don't want him to." and "I don't have to give you a reason why." Joseph was just on the last dish as he heard their footsteps coming down the stairs and dad's voice said, "Alright, Alright I'll tell him." and his mom right behind him pushing his dad and saying, "Yes, you will, listen to me, he'll be fine."

Joseph turns around to see his parents standing firmly on the ground like statues. Mr. Louis on the left with a smirk and Mrs. Louis on the right with the biggest smile. Mrs. Louis hits her husband with her left elbow on his right arm still with her smile and whispers, "Tell him."

Mr. Louis begins speaking, but is stopped by his wife, "Umm, well son, I have decided to change my mind…."

"YOU'RE GOING TO COVINGTON AFTER ALLLLL!!!!" Mrs. Louis shouts with her arms wide open, accidentally hitting her husband in the chest in the process.

Joseph's eyes lit up, "SERIOUSLY?" He throws the drying cloth on the counter in excitement.

"Jeez Nancy, let me finish." Mr. Louis says as

he knocks his wife's arm off his chest, smiles at

his son and walks back in the direction of

upstairs.

"SORRY HONEY!!! *chuckle*" Mrs. Louis says

as she goes to hug her son.

CHAPTER THREE:

THE CHANGE!!!

Monday morning comes and Joseph is in the

office of his soon to be school. The principal

hands him his new uniform. He goes to the

restroom to change; leaving his parents and

the principal to talk. The principal was an older

woman who looked as though she was there

for some years. Her name was Mrs. Colley and she had a mole on her face the size of Texas. She had on gray glasses and wore her hair in a bun with a braid around it. Her outfit resembled the student uniforms. She had on a black blazer with a blue dress and black heels. Mrs. Louis decided to wear a sleeveless red dress with gold jewelry and her usual black heels. Her husband, Mr. Louis, complemented her with his red dress shirt, black tie and dress pants and gold cross necklace that went over his tie.

"I hope I see Terry." Joseph says to himself as he wanders the hallways of Covington.

He noticed how quiet and clean the hallways were compared to his old school and the displays on the walls showed students' achievements and more and that was another thing he loved. It was his first time being inside the school, so he did not know where the restrooms were. As he proceeded to walk through the hallway to find the restroom he encountered one kid, a guy, who looked as though he was frightened by Joseph, a scared little boy; brown short hair with glasses. This kid walked faster than a chicken on a farm and when he approached him at the corner the child went on his way with two textbooks in his hand; no shoes, just his blue socks. He had no book bag which was strange to Joseph, his uniform and hair were ruffled up as if he just came from out of the jungle and he had to battle with a guerrilla.

When the boy left, Joseph continued in the direction from which the boy came from and when he turned the corner, there it was the restroom. Joseph walked in and spotted three guys who were on their way out. One student was Chinese and the shortest of the three, he looked as though he was the leader of the group, smart, dependable, bossy, and so on. The one on the right of the leader was an African American guy who did most of the beating because he was the biggest and the strongest of the three. The one on the left was a brunette who was taller and skinnier than the other two and did not do well in school as you could tell by his blank look on his face. Joseph walked into the restroom but was pushed down by the leader who was holding a book bag.

They just laughed as they exited the restroom. He waited until they were gone to get up and go into one of the blue stalls to change; he found the scared boy's shoes in one of the stalls

Joseph heard the bell ring when he was leaving. When he walked out of the restroom all the students were in the hallway, some walked to their next class, while others stood at their locker. There were a lot of students, but Joseph spotted Terry from the other side. Terry still was wearing her pigtails standing at her locker talking to two other students. One of the girls was a curly redhead with a ponytail and a bang in the front. She was the same height as Terry and stood on the right side of her. The other girl was at the open locker beside

Terry's, she was an average height girl with short straight blonde hair who wore it in pigtails on top and hair down in the back and had her nails painted with pink sparkly paint. Joseph walked through the crowd to get to Terry.

"Hey Ter!" Joseph says when he reaches the girls with his right hand raised as though he was saying an oath.

Terry turns her head to the left and does not believe her eyes. Her friends turn to look at Joseph as well. "Joe?" she says with her hands on her hips. Terry goes to hug Joseph.

"Joseph! What are you doing here?"

"I go here now," Joseph says to Terry with a smile.

"Oh really, that's great," Terry says.

"Well duh Terry, what do you expect, he's wearing our school uniform." The redhead walks over to him chewing gum. "Hi, I'm Isabella, but you can call me Bella if you like." She smiles and holds her hand out for him to shake it.

"Oh, hi Bella, I'm…" Before Joseph could shake Bella's hand and introduce himself, the blonde jumps in. "I'm Cristina, and your name is Joseph, we've heard a lot about you." She says with a smile as she closes her locker.

Joseph turns to look at Cristina and puts his hand down and Bella folds her arms and turns to look at Cristina as well. "Really? Wow, well hi Cristina." Joseph says as he waves his hand with happiness.

In all this Terry just looks at her two friends in remorse and suddenly starts laughing when Joseph finishes talking and says, "Oh yeah, ha-ha." She takes Joseph by the hand and walks him to the side of the lockers to talk to him in private.

"So, what class do you have first? I hope it's with me." Terry says in excitement.

"I don't know yet; I was just on my way back to the office to get that information. My parents are there; they would love to see you," says Joseph.

"Oh, I can't. I have to head to English, sorry maybe next time though, or I can just come over later today and I can see them when they get home and sorry again for not coming over

Friday, I had a talent club meeting. You should

totally join it." Terry says.

"It's all good, alright, I'll see ya when I see

yah," Joseph says with a smile.

"Okay, see ya when I see yah. *Chuckle*"

Terry says as she waves goodbye to Joseph.

As he walks away from Terry he turns and

says goodbye to the others. "Nice meeting you

two, Bella and Cristina."

"Nice meeting you too." Bella and Cristina say

back to Joseph.

Joseph walks back to the office and sees

his parents shaking the principal's hand. They

walk out of the office to approach him. His

mom is holding a green folder and reaches

inside of it and hands him a white sheet of

paper with words on it that say: SCHOOL

SCHEDULE. The principal walks from behind her desk, leaves her office, and closes her door and greets Joseph with a smile as his parents say their goodbyes for the day.

Mrs. Louis squats down, takes the clothes he was wearing earlier from him, and fixes up Joseph's outfit and tells him, "Alright Joey this is it. You are going to tour the school with the principal today and probably take a class. I hope you like it. Let me know when I get home tonight." She rises and grabs Mr. Louis' hand and nods at Joseph with a smile.

"Yes ma'am, will do," Joseph says as he looks up at his mom in command mode.

"Okay buddy, we have to go, but fill us in later." Mr. Louis says pointing at Joseph as he and Mrs. Louis walk away.

Joseph turns around to face his parents as they walk towards the doors, "Okay dad, no problem." He says with a thumbs up.

"WE LOVE YOU!!!" the two say as Mr. Louis opens the front office door to let his wife out first.

Joseph turns back around to see the principal still standing there with her hands together in front of her.

"Now, are you ready for the tour?" She says as she walks up to Joseph, turns him around, and walks him through the doors. They make a right into the next set of doors and make another right into the hall with the set of lockers where Terry's was earlier. They come to a stop and Mrs. Colley begins to speak.

"Here are the lockers that the kids use, there are more of them in every class hall." She says as she gestures to the lockers. "Come along now, here is the first class you will observe."

The two walk to the second classroom on the right. The Principal opens the door and lets Joseph walk in first. He enters a math class full of students, boys, and girls. The room was colorful with math puns, posters, and all. The teacher stood by her desk as a kid was standing at the board with his back to the class.

"These will not be your classmates, but this will be your first class and teacher." Mrs. Colley whispers to Joseph. The teacher teaching was a young blonde lady, much of similar age to Mrs. Vowel. She wore a white and red striped dress with a small red cardigan. Her hair was in a bob and her heels were red. She had on red lipstick and red fingernail polish. Her name was Ms. Sugar.

Joseph and Mrs. Colley walked in and entered from the back of the classroom where the students were sitting. They were learning fractions and Ms. Sugar and the student at the board were doing a problem where he had to multiply. Joseph recognized the kid, it looked like the same boy he passed in the hallway earlier that day, the one who wrestled the guerrilla, yeah, the frightened one. He worked that problem out like it was a piece of cake and when he was done he turned around and looked at the class with a smile on his face. Joseph looked at him in confusion because he was completely fine, his hair, clothes and all.

He was even wearing shoes too. That

completely got to Joseph so much that he

yelled out and interrupted the class.

"YOU'RE COMPLETELY FINE!!!!" Joseph says

as he points his finger directly at the student

from the back of the room behind the other

kids. Ms. Sugar, the whole class and Mrs.

Colley immediately looked at Joseph in shock

for they did not know what he was talking

about. "Your, your, your hair is fine, your

clothes are fine and YOUR SHOES, you have

shoes." Joseph said in panic as he paced back

and forth in front of Mrs. Colley.

"Calm down Joseph, please. Will you stop, you

do not know what you are talking about." Mrs.

Colley says in anger.

"Oh, I don't know what I'm talking about..."

Joseph says looking up at Mrs. Colley trying to

make his point.

"No, you don't," Mrs. Colley says, looking down

at Joseph in assurance.

 "Really, oh I don't know, okay well why…"

Joseph says as he puts his hands on his hips

in frustration.

"Sorry I'm late," a kid says walking into the

classroom with his clothes and hair ruffled up

with no shoes on; standing beside Mrs. Colley

and Joseph as they paused their argument to

look at him.

Everyone looked at the boy who entered. The

whole class is in dead silence.

"You were saying?" The boy at the board said

as he crossed his arms.

The guerrilla wrestler walked out of the classroom with Mrs. Colley and Joseph. Mrs. Colley told him to go to the office while she takes Joseph to his next class.

"Go to the office Franklin, while I take Joseph to Mrs. Rain's classroom, I'll be there in a minute." She turns to look at Joseph as Franklin leaves to go to the office.

"Your shoes are still in the …. bath…room." Joseph attempts to tell Franklin as he walks off.

"Don't worry, I'll get them for him. Next stop English." Mrs. Colley says as they walk straight through the hall towards the corner by the restrooms. The two continue straight until they come across a classroom with the door open.

Before they entered Mrs. Colley whispers to Joseph.

 "This will be your second block, classmates and teacher, good luck."

Joseph enters first with the principal behind him. He walked in and straight ahead as you entered was the teacher's desk sitting facing the door. He walks through and sees all the students reading books. The walls are not decorated, but under the board, in the front of the room, three little posters that explain compound sentences and other grammar rules were placed beside each other. There was Terry right in the front seat of the classroom who was deep into her book but looked up and smiled when the principal began to talk.

"Hello everyone, this is Joseph, our newest student." She turns her body right to look at Mrs. Rain who was just sitting at her desk with a book in front of her. Mrs. Rain was a middle-aged, tall, skinny, African American with short natural hair. She wore a striped, long-sleeved, white and navy-blue top with a navy blue, long skirt with black shoes. She had a glasses necklace around her neck, a red belt, and red earrings and bracelets.

"I have to go take care of another one of our students, so Mrs. Rain, I must leave him with you."

"Ahhh no problem Mrs. Colley." She says as she gets up out of her seat and joins the two at the front of the classroom.

"We are going to welcome Joseph with open arms, right guys." She says as she puts her arm around Joseph and squeezes him tight giving him a side hug.

Some students said yeah or yes while others just stayed glued to their books not caring at all. Joseph just looks up and smiles at Mrs. Rain as she is squishing him and then looks at the class with uncertainty, but suddenly he notices Terry and waves at her with his left hand. Mrs. Colley exits and Mrs. Rain points Joseph to his seat. As they walk all the way to the back of the classroom; Terry watches Joseph as Mrs. Rain talks to him.

"Here is your seat son. We are in our reading time, so you can grab a book right here." She says as she points at the bookshelf in the back behind Joseph. He walks over to the bookshelf as Mrs. Rain walks back to her desk. He starts at the top, looking for the perfect book to read. As he is busy looking for a book; Terry decides to turn back around to face the front of the classroom and puts down her Ramona Quimby classic on her desk to reach under her seat to grab SO BE IT by Sarah Weeks. She gets up from out of her desk and walks over to Mrs. Rain.

"Hey, Mrs. Rain." She whispers to her teacher. Mrs. Rain lifts her head from looking at her phone which was inside her open book.

"Yes sweetie, what can I help you with?" Mrs. Rain whispers as she takes her glasses off and lays them on her chest and sets her book and phone on her desk.

"Nothing really, I just would like to know if I can go to the back and return my book," Terry whispers with a grin.

"Oh okay, yeah sure, go ahead." Mrs. Rain says in a fast-paced way as she puts back on her glasses and grabs her phone.

Terry walks to the back of the classroom to the bookshelf. Joseph is still searching for a book to read as she arrives. She taps him on the shoulder and begins to whisper to him.

"Here you go."

"GAAA!!!" Joseph is startled.

"SHHHHH!" Terry says with her finger to her lips.

"Oh, it's just you Ter." he says as he places his hand on his chest in relief.

"You can read this one." She whispers to him as she hands him the book.

"Oh. Thanks" Joseph says as he takes the book from Terry and smiles at her.

"No problem, but inside voices, people are trying to read." She whispers as she points her hand to the class. "Before you sit down you need to sign the book out on that sheet of paper right over there," Terry says as she points at the clipboard with the white sheet of paper on top of the bookshelf. "You have to put your name, date, and name of the book. I'm going to sit down now, enjoy it." Terry whispers as she walks away. "Okay," Joseph whispers to Terry. He goes over to the clipboard and takes it down from the shelf in an attempt to write the information down. He does not know what the date is, so he glazes around the classroom to find it. Finally, he taps a kid that is sitting right in front of the bookshelf in the back. It's a nice sweet little girl by the name of Gretchen, she has a long colorful head, meaning she dyed her hair like a rainbow threw up on it. She turned around and said with the biggest smile on her face, "It's Monday, February 3rd, almost Valentine's Day." After saying thank you he finished writing down the information then walked over to his seat to read. As he is reading the intercom goes off. It's Mrs. Colley speaking: "May I have Johnny Fang, Greg Russell, and Bruce Langhart to the office, please. Thank you."

Suddenly, three guys stood up, it was the three guys from the restroom. Joseph looked over and there they were walking right out of the classroom. No one paid them any mind, not even Terry. She was deep into Ramona the Pest. Mrs. Rain looked up from her phone for a moment to see them leave. Joseph saw that no one else was paying attention, so he just continued to read.

English class was over and it was time for lunch. When the bell rang Joseph remained in his seat. He was deep into his book and didn't want to stop. Terry walked up to him so they could go to lunch. They made it to the cafeteria and Terry became swamped with friends. Joseph had no choice but to sit with them; he didn't know anybody else.

"You already know Bella and Cristina, but these are my other friends; Jeremy, Noah, and

Peter. Franklin went home early; he's Peter's twin." Terry says as Joseph takes his seat beside her.

"Well nice to meet you guys," Joseph says nervously.

"Yeah, nice to meet you, man." Jeremy responds

"Nice to meet you," Noah says.

"Already met," Peter says as he takes a bite of his apple.

Cristina and Bella walk over to join them

"You should totally be a part of our club. I'm sure we can find a spot for you." Bella says.

"He said he'll think about it guys." Terry jumps in.

"Well, we have a meeting today after school. Just come by if you want." Jeremy recommends.

The end of the day came and Joseph could not believe it. They had lunch after English, then Social Studies and Science. Joseph enjoyed his day and even got a locker right across from Terry's. They ended their day with Talent Club in the multipurpose room. The club leader was Mrs. Pug, also his science teacher. A short lady who had her black long wavy hair pulled back in a ponytail. A Native American woman who dressed like a lab professor with her white collared long-sleeved dress shirt and gray skirt and black shoes. She wore black glasses, but no jewelry at all.

Joseph joined the Talent Club and was placed to cover science, since Franklin, the guerrilla wrestler, couldn't make it to rehearsal. There were now seven members in the Talent Club, the other four included Jeremy, who covered dancing. Jeremy was a mixed guy who kind of resembled the famous singer Bruno Mars. He could not sing like him, but he sure could dance like him. As soon as he walked into the multipurpose room he went to a corner and started to rehearse his break dancing robot routine. Cristina was the singer of the group. She won almost every singing competition in the talent club. She came in doing her vocal exercises singing "Do-Ray-Mi-Fa-So-La-Te-Do Do-Ray-Mi-Fa-So-La-Te-Do" Noah on the other hand enjoyed covering history. He was a tall skinny brunette; an awkward dude with circle framed glasses. He was quiet, but once it was time to talk about history he was the most talkative person in the room. Peter was a spelling whiz; he came in there with his dictionary that he wrote himself for practice. And then there was Bella, the artist of the group; she could draw anything she tried. She walked in with some canvases and a suitcase full of all her art supplies.

The club came together every Monday and Friday to practice and to see everyone's progress. Joseph enjoyed it even though he did not officially have a category to himself yet. Franklin came to the meeting that Friday and Joseph was left to do nothing, so he just sat in the corner watching everyone do their own thing.

Mrs. Pug walked into the multipurpose room with excitement. As she wore the same lab coat and a blue button-down collared shirt with a black skirt.

"Hello everyone, I just noticed that there will be another category this year." Everyone stopped what they were doing and joined her in the center of the room. Joseph was fiddling with his thumbs and noticed everyone walking towards Mrs. Pug so he followed. She was holding a white envelope and as she opened it she said, "And the new category is going to be…" She read it to herself searching for the news. "COOKING!!!" she yelled as she raised up the letter to the sky. "Well culinary to be exact."

This was Joseph's chance to put his cooking to the test. "Mrs. Pug." Joseph said as he raised his hand. "I would like to take up the cooking portion if you don't mind." He said as he walked over to Mrs. Pug while everyone else went back to work.

"Oh, I was just getting to that, of course, you can Joseph, it would only be fair because you just joined and everyone else already has their portion." Mrs. Pug says with carelessness as she crosses Joseph to walk over to Noah. Joseph turns around in confusion. "Wait, but you don't even care if I can cook…"

"…He'll do it Mrs. Pug." Terry says as she runs from behind Joseph and pulls him by the arm.

She turns Joseph around to talk to him with a straight face. "Just be happy that they added that category or else you would not be participating, okay." She begins to smile. "Also, do your best because I know your best, you'll be fine. I got to go practice some more equations, so I'll see ya when I see yah." Terry says and proceeds to walk away to her station leaving Joseph split in the middle of the room with nothing, but starvation for work.

The competition was only a month away and that meant not a whole lot of time for Joseph to learn and practice his cooking skills. Monday the 10th came around and the school was surrounded by pink. Joseph stood by his locker and watched as girls with baskets swept the hallways. He recognized Gretchen from behind as she was standing talking to another guy and girl while holding a basket of her own. He taps her and says, "Hey Gretchen, what are the baskets for?"

"Valentine's silly." She laughs, "Sorry, I forgot you're new, they're Valentine's rose grams, see." She says as she holds out the basket showing Joseph the heart cards and roses. "Do you want one? You can write a note to your Valentine and pick a rose out. It'll be delivered on the day of Valentine's Day, which is Friday and that night will be our Valentine's Dance." She points to the big banner above the group of lockers that includes Terry's. Joseph looks at the banner then down at Terry who was talking to her friend Cristina, "Uhhhh...." He can barely speak "Uhhh.... I'll get back to you on that one." He says as he looks down and then up at Gretchen.

"That's okay, we'll be out around this time every day until the 13th," Gretchen says as she smiles and walks away.

Joseph looks back at Terry one last time before closing his locker to head to class. Terry turns her head to notice Joseph; Cristina and her walk over to him, "Hey Joe, what up." She says.

"Oh, hey Terry and Cristina, um, I better head to class, see you all in there," Joseph says as he walks away.

CHAPTER FOUR:

PRACTICE MAKES PERFECT

Every day he came home and either watched the Food Network all day or would be in the kitchen making something new. He was getting better and if the dish did not turn out perfect like he wanted it to; he would often get frustrated and throw it in the garbage. He wasted a lot of ingredients because it did not always turn out like the pictures, but something else was in his way and his mom noticed it when she came home Tuesday night. Joseph's mom did not see Terry for the second night in a row and that's when she started to ask questions.

"Hey, I'm home grumpy, what's wrong?" Joseph's mom says as she walks into the kitchen wearing a black, plain dress with black heels holding her purse. It looked like the floor was covered in lasagna. Joseph turns around with tomato sauce on his face wearing his striped shirt and khakis.

"Are you going to answer me or just stare?" She says.

"I'm sorry mom, I'm just feeling a little scared about something that I do not want to talk about especially with you." He says as he passes his mom to go sit on the couch.

"What, why not?" She joins him on the couch.

He turns to look at his mother, "If I tell you, do you promise not to tell dad about this and stay out of it?"

"Well……" She says.

"Mom." He argues.

"Fine, I won't intervene," She says with laughter.

"I'll take it. Okay, you know Valentine's Day is Friday, right?" He asks.

"Yeah, and your father better be home for that. That's beside the point, go on sweetie." She says with assurance.

Joseph stands to walk behind the couch as he says, "Well, there is this thing they call Valentine's Gram that'll be delivered that day and on top of that there is a dance too." He speeds up his words and closes his eyes, "IwanttogiveonetoTerryandaskhertothedance,b utI'mscaredto." He opens them to see his mom.

She gets up and holds his hands and talks in a calm voice, "Joseph, you shouldn't be scared, but I can see why. She's your best friend, but I have an idea of how you can do both without talking." She smiles.

Wednesday comes and Joseph is at school again. As he closes his locker he sees Gretchen walk by with the basket, "Hey Gretchen, I would like to put in Valentine's Gram now." He picks a rose, a pink one and makes his gram out to Terry. Friday comes and there is Joseph at his locker again watching various girls hand out Valentine's Grams and there is Terry standing at her locker with her two friends Cristina and Bella as Gretchen walks over to them and hands her a rose. Gretchen looks back at Joseph with a smile and thumbs up as she walks away. Terry takes the rose and opens the card that says, will you be my Valentine and go to the dance with me?

signed Joseph. She looks up in shock, looks at

her two friends, and then at Joseph and then

back at her friends with a big smile. She walks

over to Joseph with the rose in her hand.

"I would love to be your Valentine and date to

the dance. It's a yes." She hugs him and

thanks him for the rose, she locks arms with

him and they walk over to Cristina and Bella;

they all talk amongst themselves in excitement.

After school Joseph runs to his room to find a

black tux, dress shoes, socks, and a white shirt

on his bed. Dad walks shortly behind him, "I

hope you like it, mom said something about

dancing tonight, I don't know much about

dances but I know you dress nice at them." He

smiles. Joseph hugs him and then asks,

"Where's the tie?" Mom walks in holding a pink bow tie in one hand and a pink neck tie in the other.

Moments go by and there comes Joseph down the stairs. His dad is in the kitchen making himself a turkey sandwich while his mom is on the couch watching Criminal Minds. They look over to see Joseph. His mom shoots up to meet him at the bottom of the stairs to fix his bow tie.

"Looking good kid." His dad says leaning against the kitchen entrance biting into his turkey sandwich.

"Thanks, dad and mom." He says as he starts walking towards the door.

"Where are you going?" mom asks.

"To see Terry to let her know I'm ready so her dad can take us to the dance." He says as he walks out.

"Wait," Mom says as she fiddles through her bag on the lampstand to get her phone.

Joseph walks over to Terry's house, the house next door, and knocks. A large African American man answers wearing all black but with a red necktie greeting Joseph, "Hello Joseph, Terry will be down soon, come on in."

The house was decorated in pink and red with the smell of sweet perfume. Terry's mom comes down from the staircase wearing a red sparkly dress and when she stepped out the way Joseph saw a beautiful gem that was Terry wearing a pink ballerina-like dress with black heels, holding a small shoulder purse. It was slow motion in Joseph's eyes.

"Hey Mrs. Jones, you look niiiiccceee…" He was frozen, lost with words when he saw Terry.

"Hey, Joe, or should I say, Louis Joseph Louis." She laughs.

"Ohhhh… yeah, uhhhhahaahha, funny," Joseph says nervously as he locks arms with Terry to walk her out. All four were met with Joseph's mom holding up her phone recording the moment they walked out the Jones' house. They took a couple of photos before they were off to the dance. They danced the night away and had an amazing time until the rowdy ruff boys ruined it. Johnny, Greg, and Bruce came waltzing in pushing couples dancing aside. They were dressed in baggy clothes, Johnny had red and gray on, Greg had black and blue while Bruce wore green and brown. The music stopped when they met up with Franklin and his twin sitting in the corner by the punch.

"Hey Freaks!!!" the leader Bruce says.

"Hiiiiiii guys...hooooowwww arrreee youuuu doooinggg?" Franklin hesitates to say.

Everyone in the room turns to look at what is going on and suddenly Johnny lifts Peter, Franklin's twin.

"How about you ask our fist," Johnny says.

"Not the face not the face…" Peter panics as he tries to block himself from being hit.

Then a voice from the crowd speaks, "PUT HIM DOWN!!!" It was Joseph with a balled fist coming from the center of the other students walking up like the students were the red sea and they parted making Joseph Moses. Terry stood in ahhh like everyone else as Joseph walked steadily towards the boys in anger.

"I said put him down." Joseph remarks.

"AND IF HE DOESN'T!!!" Greg yells as he walks up close to Joseph. Still Peter in the air he says, "It's okay dude, I'm fine really."

"You may be fine, but your friend here is looking a little parched, let me fix that." Bruce laughs and picks up the punch bowl, "Move out of my way Greg," and pours the punch on Joseph's head, soaking him in the red liquid. "HAHAHAHA, now you're not so tough, are you? A new kid needs to learn his place around here." Bruce says as he walks away, "come on boys, this party is lame anyways." Johnny drops Peter to the ground. Bruce roughly pets Joseph's head and Greg jumps at the twins to make them flinch and follows behind Johnny. Joseph tries to jump back at them, but Jeremy runs to stop him and that's when Joseph turns around at everyone to see the fear in their eyes. "Yay for Joseph, let's get this party back in motion," Bella says as the music starts back up with everyone cheering and she starts dancing. Terry leaves the crowd to comfort him, "You were brave and that's all that matters. If it wasn't for you they wouldn't have left."

"She's right, he would have murdered my brother," Franklin says as he helps Peter up.

"Yeah, I would have been a goner for sure," Peter says as he dusts himself off.

"You all are missing the point, look at me, I didn't stand up to no one. You shouldn't have stopped me, Jeremy." Joseph says before he runs out of the party. When he makes it home he runs up to his room, slams the door, and leaves his parents downstairs on the couch in their pajamas wondering what happened.

CHAPTER FIVE:

THE COMPETITION

Monday comes back around.

"It is only two weeks before the competition and we look like amazing guys. I know you all will make me proud. Terry, can you let Joe know how excited I am for his category too as well." Mrs. Pug says as she exits the multipurpose room leaving the kids to their practices.

"Yes ma'am, of course, I am sure he just wanted to practice baking and cooking at home today."

Joseph lays on his bed in sorrow when he hears a knock on his bedroom door.

"Who is it? I'm naked and afraid to answer it." He says.

"It's me Terry."

"And me Bella."

"And Cristina."

"And Jeremy."

"And Noah."

"And your favorite twins, Franklin and Peter."

"Go away please," Joseph says as he turns back, placing his face on his pillow.

All seven walk in to see Joseph laid out on the bed.

"Why are you in my room? How did you get into my house?" Joseph asks.

"Your mom let us in. She picked us up from school." Terry says.

"Well, you all can leave now that you know I'm alive," Joseph says.

Jeremy replies as he sits on the bed beside Joseph, "Come on dude, we need you for this competition man. I know the whole punch dump was extreme, I get it, but man, you are a hero whether you realize it or not. Seeing you stand up to those dudes was brave and we commend you for that. We are your support group whether you like it or not, the dancing J, which is me of course, the know it all Noah, Christina Aguilera, that Bella girl, the twins and your girlfriend got you."

"She's not my…" Joseph was interrupted.

"Anyways…What the 'dancing J' is trying to say is that we love you and appreciate you," Terry says as she holds out her arm to get Joseph out of bed.

"So, get up and make our food, we're starving, we came here straight from rehearsal," Noah says.

Joseph laughs as he gets out of bed, "Thanks guys, so what are we standing here for, let's go cook."

The Friday night before the competition came and so Joseph made a batch of blueberry muffins for his team to wish them luck before the match and as usual, everyone loved it. When Joseph got there; his parents sat in the second row in the middle next to Terry's parents. As Joseph walked over to his group standing in the front next to all the other school teams he gave the fans a wave. The teams wore their school uniforms or their club uniforms to the competition, but a couple of them received different clothes that either added or completely changed what they were wearing for their category.

Joseph was one of these couples. He got a Toque Blanche (traditional hat), whute double-breasted jacket and hounds tooth-patterned, black and white pants for his cooking competition. Bella was given a white apron for when she painted and Cristina brought a change of clothes for her singing performance. Terry was the first one up and she was competing against three other schools. The first one to answer the twenty Algebra problems and get all right in forty minutes wins. Terry was getting it, but not fast enough. When a Hispanic girl by the name of Nana finished all twenty questions with ten minutes to spare

Terry panicked and kept looking back at Nana as she was getting corrected. When Terry saw Nana get three wrong; Terry sped up and kept up her pace to win with only two problems left and so did the other two students competing against her. Terry finished in the nick of time with two minutes left and got them all right.

"SHE GOT THEM ALL RIGHT!!!!" said the head man with the gray suit and tie.

The crowd cheered and so did Covington. It was the first competition of the day and it was just the beginning. Before Joseph knew it; it was his turn to shine for his school.

The cooking competition has started and there are three other contestants at their cooking stations. A man walks on stage and begins to speak, "And now, we have our cooking competition. The students must make a Maple glazed chicken thigh, along with vegetables and a starch of their choosing. The ingredients are at their stations; they have an hour to make this dish. Ready, begin." The man walked off stage when the timer was set. Joseph and the other students start cooking.

Joseph preheats the oven at 350 degrees and starts cleaning his chicken inside of the sink and while he is doing so he turns to look to his left and notices a familiar face. It was Mark from his old school. The same Mark that he attacked for supposedly taking his headphones. Mark was pouring broccoli into a small pot and because he was lifting his arms you could see a private school outfit under his white jacket; it was white and red. Joseph quickly turned his head back to focus on his food. When Joseph was done cleaning his chicken breast, he placed them on a pan and then decided to use green beans instead of broccoli, he poured that into a small pot just like Mark did, but didn't turn on the eye yet. He grabs a small bowl from one of the bottom drawers and pours in, 1 tbsp. of Garlic, 1 tbsp. of Ginger, fresh, ¼ cup of Maple Syrup, ½ tsp of Black pepper, freshly ground, 1 tsp Apple Cider Vinegar, and 2 tbsp. Coconut aminos. He mixes the ingredients and sets it on the counter and places the chicken into the oven to begin cooking. He sets a timer for ten minutes and begins on the rice. He pours white rice into another small pot equivalent to the green beans pot and turns that eye on med./five.

Joseph grabs the onions and as he grabs them he could hear Terry cheering him on, "GO JOE!!!" It made him smile, but then he looked over at Mark who decided to pour his mixture on top of the chicken before he placed it into the oven. It made Joseph worry a bit, but he proceeded to drop the onions into his green bean pot and turn the eye on med./five as well. Joseph looks up and witnesses his father getting out of his seat walking to the back as if he was leaving. Joseph becomes confused, so he decides to run off stage after his father. A few people from the crowd stood up and watched Joseph as he left including his family and friends. Mark even stopped in concern for Joseph, but the other two just looked up for a glance and went back to work. The judges just watched Joseph go and continued looking at their clipboards.

"Joseph, where are you going?" Terry says as she gets up from out of her seat and runs after Joseph with his mom following right behind her.

Joseph reaches his father in the hallway, "Dad."

"Joseph? You should be out there making us proud." Joseph's dad says.

"How can I make you proud when you aren't even here to watch?" Joseph says with sadness.

Joseph's dad walks up to him and bends down and places his hand on his shoulder, "Son, just because I don't see it all does not mean I won't be proud of you regardless. I know what you can do and what you have done is amazing, so go out there and do your best and even if you don't win, you are a winner in my eyes." He hugs Joseph, stands up and kisses his son on the head and smiles at him.

Joseph says, "Thanks dad…"

Before Joseph could finish, a young blonde woman enters, maybe in her 20's with a short red beautiful dress, "Hey Georgie, I'm here, we can go now."

Joseph's dad tells her, "Okay, I'm coming."

Mr. Louis attempts to leave when Joseph says, "Who's that?"

"Oh, ummm…she's a work friend." Mr. Louis says.

The lady notices Joseph and walks up to him when Terry enters the hall, "Oh, hi, you must be Joseph, I'm Grace. I'm sorry for your loss.

Your mother must have been a great woman."

With confusion, Joseph says, "What?"

She holds her hand out, but Mr. Louis takes

her other hand and says, "We have to go." and

they walk out the double doors of the building.

Mrs. Louis appears behind the kids with

her hands on their shoulders.

"Bye children," Grace says as they leave.

Joseph, Terry, and Mrs. Louis walked

back, so Joseph could finish his competition.

By this time Joseph's ten minutes were up and

it was time to pour the mixture onto the

chicken, so he did and placed it back into the

oven. Joseph had to put a slice of bread on top

of his rice because he burned it and the green

beans were finished as well.

When the time was up all the students were ready. The four placed their plates in front of the judges. Mark's was first, he had broccoli as his vegetable and yellow rice as his starch. Next to his plate was Joseph's, which had green beans as his vegetable and white rice as his starch. Because Joseph's rice burned, he lost the competition and went home in tears.

When Joseph and his mom entered the house, Joseph sat on the couch and waited till his mom walked in to ask her, "Is dad cheating on us?"

"What? No, what makes you say that?" Mrs. Louis says as she sets her purse down on the coffee table and joins Joseph on the couch.

"Because...never mind, you should just talk to dad. It's probably my fault because I'm messed up." Joseph says in despair as he walks up stairs to his room.

"What? No, Joseph, wait." Mrs. Louis says with concern. She then stands up and takes her phone out of her purse to call her husband while Joseph settles down on his bed in his room and begins to cry.

Meanwhile: Mrs. Louis is calling her husband's phone and Grace answers.

"Hello." Grace answers

"Hello? Who is this?" Mrs. Louis responded in confusion.

"Who is this? You are the one who called this number." Grace says.

"I shouldn't have to answer you, what are you doing answering my husband's phone?" Mrs. Louis answers in frustration.

"Um I'm sorry 'Ma'am', but George's wife passed away a year ago, I know because I am his fiancé. I think you might have dialed the wrong number, sorry." Grace says and then hangs up.

Mrs. Louis sits down with disbelief, looks at the staircase and begins to cry.

Joseph, still sitting on his bed in his room crying, looks at his fourth-place medal around his neck and rips it off and throws it on the floor. He gets up and starts throwing random things around in his room; his clothes in his drawer, shoes, books and more. "I wish I was different. I wish I was not like this. I want to be normal." he kept saying as he made his room a disaster. His mom runs upstairs because she heard all the commotion. When she got to his door she opened it.

Joseph ran to the door and said, "I AM NEVER GOING TO COOK AGAIN!!!!" Then he slammed the door shut on his mother.

From that day forth, Joseph never cooked again.

CHAPTER SIX:

KEEP CLIMBING

(Senior Year)

The gang is now High School Seniors who have matured into eighteen year olds. Joseph is now fitter and taller because he picked up wrestling to manage his anger. He's been a part of the team since his sophomore year and it helps to get a break from his home drama. Terry is not much taller, but smarter and has been a part of Mathletes since her freshman year. Cristina is more into the school chorus, Bella paints and acts for the drama club, Jeremy has been a part of the basketball team since freshman year, and the rest of the boys; Noah, Peter and Franklin just focus on their studies.

"I'm going for it." Terry says to Cristina.

Joseph, Jeremy, Noah, Peter and Franklin walk up to Terry and Cristina sitting at the lunch table.

"Where's Bella?" Joseph says as he and the boys take their seats.

"I'm right here." Bella walks up holding a poster decorated with two boys and two girls on it, "I give you Camp School Musical." She says as she slams the poster in the middle of the table.

"What?" Jeremy asks with a puzzled look on his face.

Bella takes her seat across from Jeremy, next to Cristina, who is across from Terry who is between Jeremy and Joseph, making Noah next to Joseph, across from Peter who is next to Franklin who is beside Cristina.

"She's talking about the new play that the school is putting on that I am trying out for. I want to play Taylor from High School Musical." Terry says.

"Oh, uhh, well I'll try out for Troy then." Jeremy says as he throws up his basketball and catches it.

"What makes you want to be Troy?" Bella asks.

"I'm good looking duhh." Jeremy says as he picks up his tray, "I'm going to go sign up, catch y'all later." Jeremy leaves the seven to talk.

"I think you'll make a great Taylor Terry." Joseph says as he sticks his fork in his red rice.

"Thanks, you should sign up too. Jeremy is right, I'm about to sign up now." Terry picks up her tray to leave. "See y'all in study hall."

"Ughhh, I already signed up for Gabriela." Bella says as she

takes her poster from the table and leaves her friends sitting.

"I'm going for Mitchie." Cristina says with a smile, taking her tray away.

Noah, Franklin and Peter take their trays and leave Joseph to finish his lunch.

Free period comes for auditions and so they begin. First up was Bella for the role of Gabriella singing "When there was me and you." Then came Terry for the role of Taylor singing "We're all in this together." Jeremy decides to change his mind and go for the part of Shane from camp rock and sings "Wouldn't change a thing" and it was beautiful. Joseph was scared to try out for Troy but he wanted to impress Terry so he sang "Gotta get my head in the game." Cristina sang "This is me" for the part of Mitchie. Surprisingly Noah steps on stage.

"Hey I'm Noah and I am only doing this because my guidance counselor says I need to do something extra to go into the college of my dreams so here we go." Noah takes a deep breath and belches out the lyrics to "Camp Rock" . He sounds terrible, but it didn't phase him.

The next day came and they all gathered in the auditorium with all the other students who tried out. Even the twins came to support.

"I have decided to change the play to just focus on Camp Rock, so here is my casting list." The drama teacher, also known as Mrs. Sam, stood to her feet from the audience chair to read the roles. She was a short ginger lady.

"Sasha will play Lola Scott." Mrs. Sam began

"Yes!" An African American girl with curls says as she high-fives the students next to her.

Mrs. Sam keeps reading the list and makes it to Taylor's part, "Taylor Jones will be playing Margaret also known as Peggy. Cristinia will be playing Tess Tyler.

"I'm okay with that." Cristina says with a smile

"Noah will be Jason Gray and Joseph will be Nate Gray. Finally our leads will be played by Bella and Jeremy. See you all tomorrow." Mrs. Sam finishes

"At least I still got the lead." Bella says as she walks out.

 Rehearsal started that Monday night at six and everyone was there on time. Bella begins as Mitchie singing, "Who will I be."

Joseph's mom shows up at the school and approaches his drama teacher. Joseph is backstage talking to Jeremy when the music suddenly stops.

"Joseph, your mom is here to take you home early, she says it's important." Mrs. Sam says

Joseph and his mom make it home to find Joseph's dad sitting on the couch almost as though he was waiting on their arrival.

"What are you doing here?" Joseph asks.

"Moral support, your mother has something to tell you." Mr. Louis says.

"Okay, what is it?" Joseph turns to his mom in concern.

"Have a seat Joseph. What I am about to say will affect our lives either tremendously or it won't be that bad I'm hoping." Joseph's mom says with remorse.

"Again, okay, what is it?" Joseph remarks. She holds Joseph's hands together in hers and starts to tear up, but then she says, "George, can you tell him please?"

"Son, your mother has stage 4 lung cancer." He says.

"WHAT? First of all…" Joseph jumps out of his seat, "I am not your son anymore since you left us for Grace five years ago and second, why are you even here if you don't care about us? Mom I love you, but letting this man back into our lives will just make you feel even worse than you already do. I'm sorry, but I can't do this." Joseph marches upstairs and slams his door.

The next morning Joseph wakes up to no sign of his mom and is greeted by Grace in the kitchen.

"Why are you in my house?" Joseph asks her.

"I'm making you breakfast. George took Nancy to the hospital because she was having some complications, but they should be back shortly." Grace tells him.

"Well, tell my mom that I will be back after school to check on her before rehearsal tonight, bye." Joseph grabs a banana and leaves out the front door.

Joseph is at his locker when his teammates Bruce and Johnny walk up.

"Hey man, I heard you tried out for that play, too bad the coach is holding practice today, so you can't rehearse." Bruce says.

"What?" Joseph folds his arms and leans back on the lockers in thought. Suddenly he sees Gretchen walk by.

"Hey Joseph, whatcha up to?" She asks.

"Nothing just annoyed with life, you?" He says with sorrow.

"Oh well I'm just handing out these fliers for Prom, hopefully that'll make you feel better. Here you go, it'll be the night before the big play Camp Rock premieres." She leaves chasing other students down with fliers, "You look like a Prom go getter…"

We all know who Joseph is going to ask to Prom, but how is he going to do it this time? Joseph makes it home and as he parks his car in the driveway he notices Grace's car isn't there anymore and walks in with a big smile on his face calling his mom to let her know he was home, but when he enters his mother's room he notices an oxygen tank by her bedside.

"Mom? Is everything okay? How are you feeling?" He sees she is too weak to roll over, so he scurries to her and holds her hand. She is coughing and then decides to sit up.

"I'm fine Joseph, I'm just glad you're home sweetie. How's everything at school? What's new?" She clears her throat and takes a deep breath.

He planned on getting advice about how to ask
Terry to Prom, but he saw his mom was having
a really bad day so he just kept to himself.
"Everything is great mom, everything is great."
They just sat in silence with each other.

Joseph stood in the kitchen that evening
and decided to call his coach to let him know
he was not able to make it to practice that day
and he did the same with his drama teacher.
He had the script, so he just studied his lines at
home, so he could stay with his mom. Weeks
went by and his mom was feeling a lot better.
George, Joseph's dad, would watch his mom
for him while he attended wrestling practice
and play rehearsals. Finally she was up and
moving with her oxygen tank like it was
nothing. As much as she wanted to go back to

work she couldn't, so she just met with her clients over the phone or through video chat. Because his mom was up and moving more he was able to go back to rehearsals and because he already knew his lines' rehearsals went by pretty smoothly. Cristina was rehearsing the song "Look at me" when Terry pulled Joseph aside.

"Hey, how's your mom doing?" she whispers.

"She's great, uh, she's up and moving now so I think it's going down." He whispers back, "Um, Terry, can I say something?"

"Yeah sure, what is it?" She says.

Suddenly Joseph backs up on stage and yells, "HIT IT!" He is joined with Jeremy, Franklin, Noah, and Peter as his background dancers and starts singing Sucker by Jonas Brothers.

Her friends Bella and Cristina push Terry out in a roll chair. He sings the first verse and the chorus and they end it with all five guys opening their jackets showing white shirts with red letters. Jeremy had the "P," Franklin had the "R," Noah had the "O" and Peter had the "M" and lastly Joseph had a shirt that said "With Me?" Terry is shocked, but quickly smiles and gets out of her seat. She walks over to Joseph and says, "Of course I'll go to prom with you." She kisses him on the cheek and hugs him.

Joseph goes home with the biggest smile on his face, he meets his mom on the couch while she watches Law and Order with a kiss on the cheek and runs up the stairs, but his mom stops him.

"What are you all smiling about sunshine?" She asks.

He stops to turn around on the staircase, "Oh nothing, just something." He shrugs.

"Would it be Prom by any chance?" She questions.

"Alright fine, you got me hahaha." he makes his way down the stairs, "How did you know?"

"I'm your mother and I'm not stupid, you're a senior." She argues.

"Alright, well thanks mom,but can we leave dad out of this one, the last thing I need is him ruining something else in my life." He sits beside her.

"Yeah okay, but I am taking you tux shopping." She says.

"Fine with me, but I'm driving of course, we have a week until prom." Joseph says as he runs upstairs.

It was Saturday and Prom was Friday and the performance was that following Saturday, so Joseph had a busy weekend ahead. Him and his mom went out tux shopping and since their Prom theme was fire and ice Terry wanted to wear red. Joseph and his mom found a red suit with hints of black in it which was perfect to compliment Terry's dress. As they left the mall his mom started to slow down her walking, so they had to take a break and sit at the food court.

"Mom, are you okay? You know what, I'm going to go get the car and try to park it closer so you don't have to walk as far, just rest here

I'll be right back." Joseph leaves to go get the car and when they make it home they are met with his father's car in the driveway. Joseph quickly gets out to help his mother get to her room to rest. He goes back downstairs where his father is waiting.

"Why are you here?" Joseph asks him.

"I'm here to work out a schedule for when you go to Prom and your play, I'll watch your mom while you do those things. Now, when is your Prom again?" His dad stands at the door frame and Joseph just runs to him pushing him to go out the door.

"GET OUT OF MY HOUSE!!!" Joseph yells. He slams the door shut and starts to cry while he sits on the floor.

Prom night comes and Joseph is dressed and ready. His mom meets him downstairs with joy. She takes pictures of her son as he walks down to greet her. There is a knock on the door so Joseph goes to answer it. It's Terry looking as beautiful as ever with the biggest smile on her face.

"Hi Joe, you look great." she says.

"And you look…" Joseph couldn't find the words.

"Absolutely stunning." Joseph's mom walks from behind him with her camera, "Let me get a picture of you two." She takes the picture and hears a beep. It's the whole gang who showed up in a limo. Jeremy's head is sticking out of the sunroof.

"HEY GUYS, MY PARENTS GOT US A LIMO AND BELLA SAID YES!!!" he laughed. Terry runs to get inside the limo and Joseph hugs his mom and runs right behind her.

Joseph is dancing with Terry to Nick Jonas' Levels when his phone starts to vibrate so he answers it.

"Hey Joseph here, what up?" He was having too much fun to notice it was his dad calling.

"You need to hurry quickly, it's your mom, we are at the Morris Hospital. Grace is on her way to pick you up now." Joseph hangs up and suddenly freezes.

"Who was that? Is everything okay?" Terry stops dancing and tries to get Joseph's attention. Joseph bolts out of the crowd and immediately starts running out of the school straight to the hospital in the pouring rain. He knew where it was and also knew he wasn't going to wait on Grace to get there.

He makes it to the hospital and has to wait to see his mom because the doctors were working on her. He sees his dad, "Is she going to be okay? Is she going to be okay?" he repeatedly asks and ends up hugging his father, he begins to sob in his arms.

The next morning comes and Joseph has spent the night at the hospital and his mom is awake and feeling fine. Joseph goes in to see her.

"Hey mom, how are you feeling?" He holds her hand.

"I'm great, better I guess, just a little scared that's all. I'm sorry, I heard I ruined Prom." He sits up and fixes her oxygen tube.

"No, you didn't ruin anything important. You are what's important to me, not a stupid Prom that kept me away from you." He begins to cry and decides to give his mom a hug.

"Well the doctors say I can go see your play tonight, so I will be there I promise." She says. Joseph gets up from his hug with his mom, looks at her and says, "I love you." He kisses her on the cheek. Grace drops Joseph home to prepare for his play, they had a pre show rehearsal set for four before the main event which was set for six. Joseph drove to rehearsal happy for his mom's well-being and he didn't really care if his mom made it to the show that night because he already knew she was alright and that is what made him happy.

"My parents told me your mom was in the hospital. We visited her today, she's looking a lot better now Joe, so I think she'll be fine from here on out." Terry says.

"Yeah, the doctors say she'll be back on her feet in no time, but she'll still need the oxygen tank though." Joseph says.

It was show time and everyone was in place. Joseph's mom is brought in with her dad and Grace moments before Joseph, Franklin and Jeremy had to sing "Heart and Soul" Joseph's mom loved it and was proud of her son and Joseph was proud to see his mom.

CHAPTER SEVEN:

IT'S LIFE

(2 years later)

"WILL YOU JUST STOP…," Joseph says angrily with frustration in his voice to his mother. He is laying on the couch in his pajamas.

Mrs. Louis calmly interrupts, "No Joseph, I will not stop, I love you son, but you need to start your life and stop living off us, you need a job." Mrs. Louis was dressed for work, wearing an orange dress and black blazer. She was down to cancer stage 1 and was able to work again. Mr. Louis moved back in for good and broke things off with Grace last year.

Out of rage, twenty-year-old Joseph stands up and says, "YOU KNOW WHAT, I DON'T NEED YOU, I DON'T NEED THIS, MATTER FACT, I HATE YOU AND YOU," Joseph points at his dad who was wearing one of his usual suits, looks him straight in the eye and whispers to him, "Don't worry……I'm going to leave you like you left me and one day you'll be crying for help and guess what?"
As Joseph's dad looks down to the floor he questions his son, "What?"
Joseph spreads his arms out and answers his father with a great big enthusiastic smile on his face, "I won't come…. I WON'T COME!!!"
Joseph storms up to his room and packs his

things in a black gym bag, puts it across his body and then stomps out the house and speeds away in his car.

Joseph graduated from high school two years ago and he has yet to find a job, well, he has yet to even look for one. He didn't go to college because he lost his wrestling scholarship for wigging out at a tournament putting Bruce in the hospital. He thought he could stay with his mom so she wouldn't be lonely, but now that she's back with his father the only thing he lacks is self-control and the strive to do better. He lost contact with Terry when her family moved and she left for Harvard and his other friends went to other Universities as well. He gives up on all projects if it is not finished in a day. His parents claim he has changed and will get better, but Joseph does not think he will. He figures that all is lost and he cannot manage his anger anymore. Joseph leaves the house and continues to drive farther away from home until Jacksonville becomes Orlando. He rides as his face continues to be pelted by his tears. Night falls and all he wants to do is eat, so he stops by a Subway. When he leaves the Subway, he decides to check into a hotel, but of course they didn't allow him to stay because of his appearance, so he had to sleep in his car that night. He slept across from a gym called the YMCA, so the next morning he walked in. He walked to the front counter and spoke with a lady dressed in workout clothes and said, "Hi, am I able to take a shower here?"

“Are you a member?” The lady asked.

“Ummm….no” Joseph said with regret.

The lady looked at his clothes and smelled his odar and how messy he looked and said, “You know what, it's on me. Go ahead.”

“Oh, um thanks” Joseph walked to the bathroom and showered and got dressed. When he walked out the lady stopped him.

“Hey, you look like you need a job.” The lady said.

“Yes actually.” Joseph said.

“Well, you can have one here if you like. I know it’s nothing fancy, but it’s just to get you on your feet.” The lady said with a smile.

“Really? Oh, my gosh, thank you so much, ma’am.” He shakes her hand vigorously. “You will not regret this.”

"I hope not, just be here in the morning by eight." She said,

"Will do." Joseph leaves and goes back to the hotel to stay.

Joseph enjoyed working at the Y every day from eight in the morning to three in the afternoon. He made friends and because he worked there he had a free gym membership so he could work out when he could. Soon after he got his job a fellow employee offered him to stay with them so he wouldn't have to continue paying hotel prices. Life was finally looking up for Joseph.

One day he and a few of the YMCA employees were given the opportunity to eat at a five-star restaurant called The Grand Slam, so they went. When they arrived, there were chefs cooking in front of the guests, fine dining and music. Joseph and his friends had a blast. Joseph realized how much he wanted to try and do what the chefs did, so when he went home that night and many nights after work he practiced throwing up his knife, cooking on one of those long pan grills and more, he even made the SpongeBob out of rice. One afternoon when he got off from work, he went home, showered and got dressed and went over to The Grand Slam again, but this time it was for a job opportunity. He walked up to one of the waiters who just finished taking someone's order and put his hand out for a handshake, "Hi my name is Joseph. I was wondering if you guys were hiring any more chefs." He stood there with the biggest smile on his face.

"Well, Joseph, I can't tell you if we are or not. If you would just give me a moment, I'll be right back." The guy walked into the kitchen while Joseph just waited there passionately.

The waiter soon after called Joseph into the kitchen. When he entered, he saw about ten people; chefs, cooks, food prep workers and then a big man with the gut the size of Saturn walked out from the office wearing the red version of a chef's attire, he was the head chef, 'Sir chef' they say.

"You want to work here?" He laughed.

"Yes sir." Joseph said.

"As a waiter I'm hoping." Sir chef says.

"No sir, as one of your cooks and or food prep workers." Joseph says with confidence.

"Okay, you are on dish boy duty tomorrow, be here at seven." Sir chef says.

"In the morning?" Joseph asks.

"Yes, in the morning. See you then." Sir chef walks out the kitchen doors into the lobby to greet some guests.

The next morning came and Joseph woke up at five, showered and got dressed. He practiced what he knew by making himself a bowl of oatmeal and egg yolk on top with a small bowl of fruits and yogurt on the side. While he was enjoying his meal, he saw that he received a voicemail from his mother and instead of listening to it he decided to give her a call. It was six in the morning, so she did not answer.

"I'm sure it's nothing so I'll just listen to it later and call her another time." Joseph finished his breakfast and drove to the restaurant. He got there around 6:45 and saw that a few people were sweeping and cleaning and making sure all was well for the day. Joseph walked into the kitchen and the same waiter from last night greeted him.

"Great, you are here. You can start on these. When you are done, you can mop." The waiter took him to a sink filled with dishes from last night and left.

Joseph washed dishes all day and didn't get to mop till it was dark. His first day was a disaster, people yelled at him for pots not being washed in time and they kept giving him more and more dishes to wash and it made it impossible to be done. Joseph did not get home until two in the morning because he had to finish washing more dishes after he mopped the kitchen and cleaned the bathrooms. He was so tired, but he did not want to give up on this opportunity.

When Joseph made it home he finally looked at his phone and saw that there were about twenty missed calls from his father, but he did not call back, instead he went to sleep. The restaurant was closed on Sundays and It was a Friday, so he still had tomorrow and next week to go.

A year has passed and he finally found a place of his own. Joseph was still the dish boy, he was no longer able to work at the YMCA due to his only days off being Sundays and the YMCA was also closed on that day. Joseph would use Sunday afternoons for running and exercising at home and on the sidewalks when he could; mornings were for church service. He never contacted his father and spent his holidays alone.

One Saturday afternoon as he was working at The Grand Slam, Joseph was walking from out the kitchen to clean the men's room when he glanced over at the guest and saw a familiar face and the familiar face saw him too and got up and walked to him. It was Terry, twenty-one-year-old Terry, who was having lunch with her parents. She was wearing a lovely blue dress and a yellow sweater, her hair was straightened, she was beautiful.

"Joe? Is that you?" She said as she approached him.

"Yeah, I guess so." Joseph said with a smirk on his face.

"What are you doing here?" Terry asked

"I should be asking you the same thing, but I work here." Joseph said.

"Really, wow, do you cook the food?" Terry said with enthusiasm.

"Umm not exactly" Joseph says as he holds up the cleaning supplies.

"Oh, and I'm sorry for your loss Joseph and I am very saddened that you couldn't make it to the funeral." Terry says as she hugs Joseph.

"What are you talking about?" Joseph asked.

"Your mother passed away last year from cancer, remember? You didn't know?" Terry says with concern.

"No, I had no Idea." Joseph dropped his cleaning supplies and fled out of the restaurant.

That night he made it to his parent's house and knocked on the door and Grace answered.

"Hi Joseph, I am so happy you could make it. Want something to eat?" She said with a smile.

"No, no, this can't be happening." Joseph immediately ran off the doorstep, and drove away. On his way home he stopped by a grave site and luckily his mother was buried there. He knelt at her grave, kissed the gravestone and left a flower. That night he cried himself to sleep.

The next day after Joseph made it home from church, he decided to go for a jog. As he was jogging he had a breakdown and started to cry, he fell to his knees and screamed out loud.

"I'M SORRYYYYY!!!, I'm sorry." He put the rest of his body down and cried and cried.

Terry was jogging by and noticed him on the ground.

"Sir, are you okay?" She asked. "Sir?" She helped him to his feet and realized it was Joseph.

"Joe??? What are you doing? Oh my gosh, are you okay? Come on, sit down." She walked him to a bench that was nearby.

"Yeah, I'm fine. Can I go now?" Joseph says as he attempts to leave.

"No, you cannot, you are going to talk to me. Now dry your tears and tell me what is up." Terry demands.

"It's my mom, I can't believe she's gone." Joseph cries.

"I know it's hard, but all you can do is keep living, it's life." Terry tells him.

"You're right." He dries his tears.

"And, I'll tell you what, if you keep living, you will make your mom proud. Just keep doing you and don't worry Joey, it will all work out in the end." She says as she hugs him.

"Thanks Terry, I really appreciate it, really. Now, why are you here?" Joseph says.

"oh, my mom and dad moved here, I'm just visiting for a few days." Terry laughs. "I can see that you are doing pretty well, I mean you look good and you work at a five-star restaurant."

"As a dish boy." Joseph says with disappointment. "I bet mom is proud now."

"Hey, it's still a five-star restaurant though. Come on, my parents would love to see you." Terry says.

"Okay, but not like this, let me go shower first, text me the address." Joseph says as he hands Terry his phone, so she could put her number in.

"Okay, no problem." Terry says as she hands Joseph her phone.

After they exchange numbers Terry jogs away. Joseph got ready and found himself at the Jones' house where he is enjoying a meal with laughter and fun.

"So, Joseph, what are you doing these days' son? Terry told us that you work at The Grand Slam, where we enjoyed lunch yesterday." Terry's dad said.

"oh, um well Mr. Jones, I do work there, but I am just a dish boy for now, but hopefully I will soon be able to actually make the food." Joseph laughs.

"That's, that's good," Mr. Jones says.

"Dinner is delicious Mrs. Jones…." Joseph says, trying to change the subject.

Monday morning came and it was time for work again. When Joseph arrived at work, he went straight to the sir chef's office.

"I am so sorry; it will never happen again. There was a family emergency." Joseph pleated.

"Enough, it's alright, I don't care. You are here now and we need your help. You met Tommy, right? Well, he's one of our cooks and he's out sick today and we need a fill in. You see, the President of the United States is coming, so I need you to work swiftly and try to stay here at least till the President leaves. I am not sure what time he will be here, but we must be on our P's and Q's." Sir Chef says.

"Yes, sir chef." Joseph says and walks out of the office with the biggest smile on his face. He now could dress and work like a chef just like he always dreamed and it was all because Tom called in sick. Everyone was working at a fast pace and it was faster than Joseph could handle. There were guidelines for Joseph on the side to show him how to make every meal, all he had to do was flip through it. Joseph made about ten meals that day before the president showed up that evening for dinner.

 The President came and it was time for his order and he told the waiter to bring him whatever they give him. During the President's arrival Joseph was in the middle of making his maple chicken thigh meal that he lost at his seventh-grade food competition, to eat because he was on break. Instead of doing white rice, he made mashed potatoes and used kale instead of green beans. He was finished with the plate and ready to eat it, but then he had to go to the restroom. When he walked out of the restroom he noticed Terry sitting down at a table alone waiting to order, so he walked over to her to say hey. While Joseph was out; the waiter who was attending the President walked right into the kitchen and grabbed Joseph's meal and took it to the President. He was not paying much attention to the fact that it was not on the menu, he just grabbed the first meal he saw at the line up on the counter.

"I see you are here to visit me again." Joseph says as he walks over to Terry, who was wearing one of the most gorgeous pink dresses with her hair curled and down, with a big smile on her face.

"Oh, hey Joey, oh my gosh, are you cooking now?" Terry asked.

"I sure am. Are you here alone?" Joseph asked.

"Umm, no, my boyfriend is in town… and there he is now. Joseph, this is…" Terry was saying as a handsome man also in his 20's with curly, blonde hair walked up behind Joseph.

Joseph interrupted her and said, "Mark, I know… I should actually hurry back now, I just wanted to say hey." Joseph says as he walks away.

 "Oh… okay, nice seeing you, and good luck." Terry says.

"Nice seeing you too Joey… ha-ha that guy." Mark teased.

Joseph made it back into the kitchen and then remembered his food, so he looked at the counter he set it on. He saw that it was missing and he was in shock and was asking everyone

in the kitchen where it had gone. The waiter

came back in and Joseph ran to him.

"Did you take it?" he said as he shook the man.

"Took what? What are you talking about?" the

waiter said.

"The food that was on that counter, the one

that had the maple chicken?" Joseph said.

"Uhhh??" the waiter said.

"THE PLATE WITH THE MASHED

POTATOES!!!!" Joseph yelled as he shook the

man one more time.

"Oh, ummm the President has it." The waiter

says with confusion.

"WHAT?!?! I made that food." Joseph says with

anger

"So, what's the big deal?" The waiter asks.

"The big deal is that IT'S NOT ON THE MENU!!!! Joseph yells and attempts to walk out of the kitchen when the sir chef walks up behind him. The waiter walks back into the lobby to attend to the President.

"Why are you yelling? Our guest will hear you, and by guest, I mean the President." Sir chef says.

"Ummm... well sir chef..." Joseph says as the waiter walks back in.

"The President would like to see the cook that made his meal, Joseph." The waiter said.

As the waiter, Joseph, and Sir chef walked out to the President, Sir Chef wanted to know which meal Joseph selected to make.

"Which one did you choose, Joseph?" Sir chef asked.

"Ummm… a new one." Joseph said with regret.

"Okay, that's fine, but which one was it though, you have to be specific…." Sir chef says as he encounters the meal that the President had displayed on his table. The President was halfway through with it when he called them out.

"That is not one of our selections." Sir Chef whispered to Joseph.

"Hello, Sir Chef, is this the cook that made this amazing meal? It was delicious, but I did not see it on display. Why is that?" The President says.

Terry and Mark look at Joseph as he answers the President.

"Well, Mr. President, sir, it's a funny story actually…" Joseph says as he looks over at Terry and Mark.

EPILOGUE

O'Tia Prioleau

I would like to first and foremost thank my Lord and Savior Jesus Christ for giving me this gift. I would also love to thank everyone who took part in the process of me getting the motivation to publish. My parents and my siblings pushed me the most and encouraged me to keep writing everyday. Poetry started my love for writing but my passion for storytelling was always there. It showed the most when I would turn on the TV. All I did was watch television growing up and I would and still will be the one who chooses the movie.

I started this story from the end back in 2016. I was just randomly writing while waiting for my father to get off work. The first thing you write won't always be the actual product. This story had an alternative cliff hanger and I'm going to give you it right now. My plan was to have Joseph become so angry at a waiter that while that waiter was about to go on his lunch break; Joseph was going to add poison to his food. The idea was to always have the president attend the restaurant but he was going to bring his dog. The waiter was going to serve the president before going on break and it was going to be the plate of food that Joseph poisoned. In the midst of trying to stop the president from eating the food; Joseph knocks the food over causing his dog to eat it instead.
I was going to leave it at that and continue the story in another book, but this cliff hanger allows more of an opportunity to expand on Joseph's journey. I withheld the fact that Joseph actually has Aspergers only because you can pick it up based on how he interacts with others. I want this story to be a lesson for everyone; just because you go

through hardship doesn't mean you should make your life hard. You can still accomplish what you set out to do; it might not go the route you intended but you'll get there eventually. It's not about the situation you're in but what you do with the situation you are in.

Remember to always be the best you can be because only you can be the best you can be.